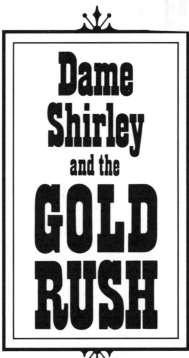

Dame Shirley
and the
GOLD RUSH

Published by Steck-Vaughn Company.

Text, illustrations, and cover art copyright © 1993 by Dialogue Systems, Inc., 627 Broadway, New York, New York 10012.

Cover art by John Holder

Printed in China
13 788 05

Library of Congress Cataloging-in-Publication Data

Rawls, James J.
    Dame Shirley and the Gold Rush / author, Jim Rawls; illustrator, John Holder.
        p.   cm.—(Stories of America)
    Summary: Relates how a series of letters, written by a woman known as Dame Shirley and published in a San Francisco magazine in 1854 and 1855, were instrumental in relating the true story of the California gold rush.
        ISBN 0-8114-7222-1 (hardcover) — ISBN 0-8114-8062-3 (softcover)
        1. California—Gold discoveries—Juvenile literature. 2. Shirley, Dame, 1819-1906—Juvenile literature. 3. Frontier and pioneer life—California—Juvenile literature. 4. Pioneers—California—Biography—Juvenile literature. 5. Women pioneers—California—Biography—Juvenile literature. 6. California—Gold discoveries. [1. Shirley, Dame, 1819-1906. 2. Frontier and pioneer life—California.] I. Holder, John, ill. II. Title. III. Series.
    F865.R29   1993
    979.4'04—dc20   92-18083
                                                            CIP
                                                            AC

ISBN 0-8114-7222-1 (Hardcover)
ISBN 0-8114-8062-3 (Softcover)

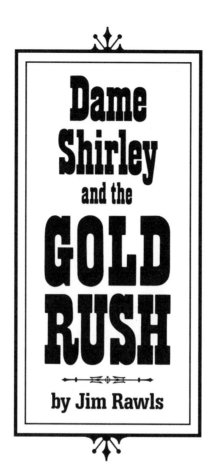

Dame Shirley and the GOLD RUSH

by Jim Rawls

Alex Haley, General Editor

Illustrations by John Holder

STECK-VAUGHN
C O M P A N Y
A Subsidiary of National Education Corporation

To Marlene Smith-Barazini, future biographer of Louise Amelia Knapp Smith Clappe

Introduction
by Alex Haley, General Editor

Writers are witnesses. They tell you what they have seen in their lives and in the world around them. The best writers surprise us with the truths they present. *Dame Shirley and the Gold Rush* is about the writer who first brought the truth about the California Gold Rush to a large audience.

It was a truth that surprised many people in the 1850s. According to the rumors of the day, gold lay thick in the riverbeds and hillsides of California's mountains. They said anyone could get rich just by heading west and picking up the gold that lay all around. Thousands chased after the rumors. The truth of what they found and what happened to them became Dame Shirley's story. It is a story of a writer bearing witness to her times.

Dame Shirley was the name used by Louise Amelia Knapp Smith Clappe when she first published her Gold Rush letters. It is as Dame Shirley that she became famous, so that is how she is referred to in our story.

Conte

Introduction
by Alex Haley, General Editor

Writers are witnesses. They tell you what they have seen in their lives and in the world around them. The best writers surprise us with the truths they present. *Dame Shirley and the Gold Rush* is about the writer who first brought the truth about the California Gold Rush to a large audience.

It was a truth that surprised many people in the 1850s. According to the rumors of the day, gold lay thick in the riverbeds and hillsides of California's mountains. They said anyone could get rich just by heading west and picking up the gold that lay all around. Thousands chased after the rumors. The truth of what they found and what happened to them became Dame Shirley's story. It is a story of a writer bearing witness to her times.

Dame Shirley was the name used by Louise Amelia Knapp Smith Clappe when she first published her Gold Rush letters. It is as Dame Shirley that she became famous, so that is how she is referred to in our story.

Contents

1

A Trip to the Mines

Dame Shirley rubbed the sleep from her eyes and pulled the coarse woolen blanket up around her shoulders. The early morning air was cool and still. She lay quietly, listening to the sounds of daybreak drifting through the cabin window. Outside, a mule brayed, and a screeching rooster saluted the rising sun.

It was early September 1851. Dame Shirley and her husband, Dr. Fayette Clappe, had spent the night at a ranch near Marysville, California. Today they were to begin their ride north along the Feather River to the gold mining camp of Rich Bar.

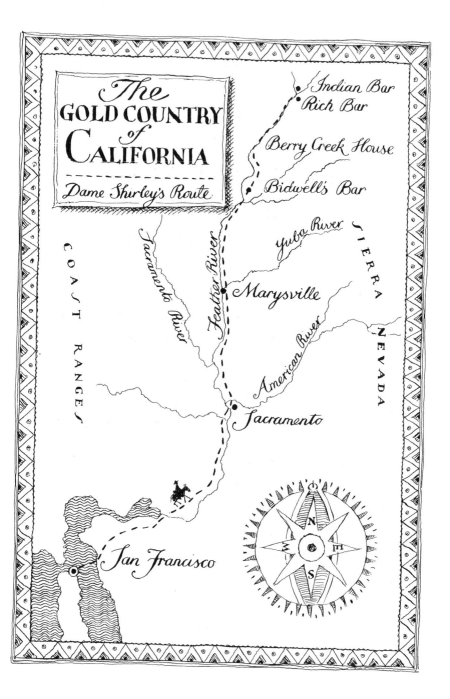

The couple had been lured to California by the Gold Rush. They were not alone. Thousands of others had come for the same reason.

Dame Shirley thought about how far they had come from their home in New England. At the time, no highways or railroads linked California with the rest of the United States. So Dame Shirley and Fayette had to sail all the way around South America to reach San Francisco—a trip of about seventeen thousand miles!

From there, they rode a stagecoach north to mining country. The stage's wooden wheels had bounced and jumped over a road that was more trail than highway. It was like being trapped for several days in a small wooden box that someone was shaking. The ride was a bit longer than one hundred miles, but seemed like a thousand.

This morning, though, Dame Shirley and Fayette were rested and ready to continue their travels.

They were going to Rich Bar to find work for Fayette. Dame Shirley and Fayette knew that Rich Bar had a population of several thousand miners. They also knew that it had just one doctor. Fayette was certain he would have plenty of opportunities to practice medicine there.

Dame Shirley pulled herself out of bed and gazed at her reflection in a broken mirror tacked to the cabin wall. Her blue eyes were still blurry with sleep. She brushed the tangles from her long hair and dressed quickly. She put on clean riding clothes and a freshly polished pair of boots. She inspected her riding hat and gloves, flicking invisible dust from both. After breakfast, she would be ready to go.

Breakfast at this ranch in the California wilderness was—to be polite—meager. Shirley and Fayette shared three or four dried biscuits. Each was hard enough to break glass. They ate several slices of salt ham that could have been mistaken for boot leather. Then they washed the meal down with some bitter green tea. Hardly a breakfast to ready one for a day on the back of a mule! Dame Shirley sipped the tea cautiously, wincing at its bitter taste. She was grateful that it only *tasted* poisonous!

She and Fayette had hoped to get an early start, but one thing or another delayed their departure for most of the day. Dame Shirley tried to be patient. She wandered out into the ranch yard. There, she passed time by giving names to each of the nearly eighty chickens, turkeys, and geese that paraded past the cabin.

At last, late in the afternoon, everything was ready, and the two travelers climbed aboard their mules. Rich Bar lay some ninety miles to the north, a ride of several days. Marysville, their first stop, was ten miles away. Dame Shirley and Fayette wanted to get there by nightfall. They nudged their mules to move faster.

Friends in San Francisco had warned Dame Shirley not to go the mines. One woman had predicted that she would never make it to Rich Bar alive. Another had said that Dame Shirley was crazy to think of living in a mining camp made up almost entirely of men. Even Fayette had advised her to remain in San Francisco. Everyone said that going to the mines was too dangerous for a woman.

But Dame Shirley would have none of it. All her life she had dreamed of travel and adventure. She once said that she was a "thistleseed," ready to blow wherever the wind might take her. She felt a restlessness in her soul. She had the spirit of a nomad. And having come so far already, she meant to experience life in the mines, not merely to hear about it from her husband or the newspapers.

Seeing San Francisco had been a grand experience. It was far different from the New England villages she knew so well. In the two years since the Gold Rush began, San Francisco had grown from a sleepy village of some eight hundred souls to a wild, teeming frontier city of twenty-five thousand people. Going to a rough-and-tumble mining camp promised even greater excitement.

Dame Shirley nudged her mule again with her foot. Then she felt a strange sensation. Her saddle was slipping! Suddenly, she and the saddle were a mini-avalanche sliding sideways off the mule. Before she knew it, she was lying in the road, a cloud of dust mushrooming around her. Her saddle swung upside down beneath her mule. Dust filled her eyes, nose, and ears. Her fine riding outfit was coated with dust.

A look of horror filled Fayette's face. He quickly dismounted and rushed to help Dame Shirley to her feet. Shirley, though, didn't need any help. She was startled, but unhurt. Getting up, she looked at Fayette. A grin spread across her face. She began to laugh.

When he went to fix her saddle, Fayette discovered that it was far too large for her mule. He could fix it so that it might hold for a bit, but he wasn't sure how reliable it would be. He suggested they turn back instead. At the very least, he said, she should return to the ranch and put on some clean clothes and make a fresh start.

Dame Shirley said no to both suggestions. She surveyed her appearance. Indeed, she was a sight. She was covered in dust, from tip to toe. But so what? This was California. This was mining country. Who on Earth was she going to run into here? Certainly not anyone who would turn up his nose at a little dust. Something about the idea of her great adventure beginning with a

little comedy pleased her. She climbed back on her mule and rode merrily on.

Fayette insisted they ride very slowly. He feared Dame Shirley's saddle might come loose again. The shadows of trees crept across the trail. Afternoon gave way to evening. Soon, only the moon and the ivory stars lit the way.

Finally, at about midnight, they reached Marysville. There they spent the night after dining on a feast of hot oysters, toast, tomatoes, and coffee. It was their first meal since breakfast.

2

Know Nothing, Fear Nothing

The next morning, Fayette awoke feeling ill. For several days he was bedridden with a fever. When he was well again, plans were made for the rest of their journey.

Dame Shirley's saddle was still a concern. They decided she would travel by stagecoach until they reached Bidwell's Bar. Bidwell's Bar was a town halfway between Marysville and Rich Bar. Fayette would take the mules and meet her there.

Early on a Monday morning, Dame Shirley boarded the stagecoach and took her seat. She was the only passenger. The driver climbed up top. As he did the wagon rocked wildly. A strange clicking sound from the driver sent the horses charging forward.

By California standards, the road through town was smooth. Still, the stagecoach bounced along like the head of a hammer repeatedly striking a table. Dame Shirley braced herself in her seat. This wagon didn't have any springs at all! She was in for an even bumpier ride than the one from San Francisco.

It was a 39-mile ride to Bidwell's Bar. This time around, Dame Shirley didn't seem to mind all the bouncing and tumbling about. In fact, she quite enjoyed it!

Maybe she had already grown used to the rough roads and bumpy rides. Or maybe it was because the first thirty miles took her through some of the most beautiful country she'd ever seen. It was like New England, but saucy and wild.

Not long after leaving Marysville, the coach passed by a group of American Indian women. They were gathering seeds from a field of wild-flowers. Dame Shirley had read many stories about Indians, but never before had she actually seen any. She marveled at the baskets the women carried and at the grace with which they worked.

As the stagecoach neared Bidwell's Bar, the road became stony and rough. The horses strained as they pulled the coach up a steep mountain slope. The road narrowed dangerously. For over a mile, the stagecoach wobbled along the edge of a steep cliff.

Dame Shirley's breath came in short gasps. One slip by the horses, and the stagecoach would topple over the edge. Waiting below were huge boulders and jagged rocks. Dame Shirley felt a scream rising in her throat. She swallowed hard and remained silent—as silent, she thought, as death.

When at last the stagecoach reached the other side of the mountain, the driver turned to Dame Shirley. "Wall," he said, "I guess yer the fust woman that ever rode over that are hill without hollering."

Dame Shirley smiled to herself. She didn't bother to say that it was fear that had kept her

so quiet. She had passed a great test. She may have been scared, she thought, but at least she hadn't shown it.

Dame Shirley arrived in Bidwell's Bar at three o'clock in the afternoon. She and Fayette had intended to spend the night, but by early evening they changed their minds. The only place to sleep was on bare ground beneath an oily canvas tent. In and out of the tent, the air was black with madly hopping fleas. They decided to ride on to Berry Creek House, a ranch ten miles away.

The moon was just rising as they headed out on the trail. Dame Shirley was relieved to be traveling by mule once again and not by stagecoach. She and Fayette sang songs and told stories as they rode along. Their laughter filled the moonlit woods.

Their mood changed, however, as the night wore on. The time had long since passed when they should have reached their destination. They were lost. Fayette tried to pretend that they weren't. Several times he assured Dame

Shirley that Berry Creek was just ahead. But it wasn't.

The trail became choked with brush. The two riders bent low over the backs of their mules. Tree limbs grabbed and scratched at them as they rode by.

They wandered higher and higher into the mountains. By two o'clock in the morning, Fayette had to admit they were hopelessly lost. Still, he wanted to keep going.

Dame Shirley had had enough. For all they knew, they were closer to San Francisco than to Berry Creek House. It made more sense to try and get some sleep. At least in the daylight, they might be able to see where they were going. To keep on in the dark would just get them even more lost.

Fayette protested, but Shirley refused to ride any farther that night.

The exhausted couple slept on a bed of pine needles. The forested hills hummed and howled with night sounds. Bears, cougars, wolves, and snakes lived in these hills. If these dangers frightened Dame Shirley, she didn't say. Perhaps she was grateful just to sleep. Tomorrow she could worry about them and about Indians and about being so lost that they might never be found. Tonight it was enough to be on soft ground. No sooner had her head touched her pine-needle pillow than she was asleep.

At dawn, barely rested and still hungry, they began their journey again. On and on they rode, up hills and down, through groves of fir and clumps of oak.

They hadn't eaten anything since noon the day before. Their bodies ached, and so did their hearts. They might die on this mountain trail.

California was still a wilderness. Rattlers, mountain lions, and grizzlies were a real danger. So were California's Indians, who were fighting to defend their land from the floods of gold seekers brought by the Gold Rush. And some of the gold seekers weren't miners—they were robbers and murderers. They'd bushwhack people like Dame Shirley and her husband, steal whatever they had, and either kill them or leave them to die in the hills.

Despite all this, the greatest danger was being lost. They could quite easily starve to death before they ever found their way again.

On and on they rode, the hot sun blazing down on them. Dame Shirley and Fayette said little. There were no songs or jokes to pass the time. They searched every space between trees, every little cut that might lead to the main trail. For long hours, there was nothing.

Finally, at two o'clock in the afternoon, they stumbled on the main trail again! They still had several hours of daylight left to get somewhere. Even Bidwell's Bar with all its fleas would have been welcome. Giddy with relief, they rode along the main trail until they met a man who gave them directions to Berry Creek House. He said they'd traveled in a great big circle. They'd gone nearly thirty miles out of their way!

The good news was that the ranch was now only about seven miles away. It might just as easily have been thirty or forty miles away! Fayette was embarrassed to learn how lost they had been. Shirley was just happy to know that in a few hours, they'd be at the ranch. They rode on as fast as their worn-out mules would carry them.

They arrived exhausted. Dame Shirley wanted to go straight to bed. A little sleep was all she wanted. Fayette tried to bring her some food. "Take it away!" she said. "Just give me some cold water and let me *sleep*, and be sure you don't wake me for the next three weeks."

But the next morning found Dame Shirley and Fayette once again on their mules. For two more days they rode on. At last, they came within sight of the mining camp of Rich Bar.

Rich Bar lay at the bottom of a steep canyon. The only way to reach it was down a narrow, rock-covered path. Dame Shirley and Fayette urged their mules forward. They tried not to look at the dim valley below.

Dame Shirley kept her eyes on the front feet of her mule. She watched it step carefully and surely among the rocks. About halfway down the slope, Dame Shirley felt her saddle begin to slide!

Not again, she thought. *Not now!* She saw herself tumbling over the edge of the path into the canyon below. But *now* was the only right time for this to happen. The saddle gave way on the only part of the trail wide enough to catch a falling body.

Dame Shirley landed on the ground unhurt. This time she didn't laugh at her mishap. She had been through too much for that. Instead, she thanked God for the saddle's good timing, and stood and gazed silently at the mining camp below.

Fayette quickly dismounted and rushed to his wife's side. Dame Shirley had a determined, expectant look on her face. He followed her gaze to the mining camp. Whatever it was his wife saw, he didn't see. All he saw was just another flea-ridden mining camp like Bidwell's Bar. He shrugged his shoulders, puzzled at his wife's fascination. Then he turned and inspected her troublesome saddle.

After mending it once again, he and Shirley resumed their journey down the rocky slope.

By five o'clock that evening, they were safely in Rich Bar. The miners were astonished to see Dame Shirley. Few women had ever made

the trip to this remote mining camp. They gathered in a noisy crowd around her. Here was a woman with gumption! A woman with sand in her britches! Dame Shirley listened to the excited words of the miners and felt enormously proud.

Shortly after arriving in Rich Bar, she wrote the first of her letters to her sister, Mary Jane. She described her trip to the mines and the great hullabaloo that greeted her arrival. Dame Shirley wrote:

I, of course, feel very vain of my exploit, and glorify myself accordingly; being particularly careful all the time not to inform my admirers, that my courage was the result of the know nothing, fear nothing principle; for I was certainly ignorant until I had passed them, of the dangers of the passage.

Her trip to the mines had been much more of an adventure than she had bargained for, yet she had survived. Her courage and determination, however, grew out of her restlessness, not her ignorance. Now her restless soul was eager for more.

3

Life in the Diggings

Fayette had been right about one thing. Rich Bar *was* just like Bidwell's Bar—and like all the other mining camps in California's gold country.

Its one main street was a dirt road. During the long, dry summer months the road was rock hard and dust covered. Come the rainy days of winter, it turned into a river of mud. Miners and mules would get swallowed up to their knees by the muddy road.

Dame Shirley counted about forty buildings in Rich Bar. Most were canvas tents. Others were plank sheds or log cabins. How different it was from the comfortable little towns Dame

Shirley had known in New England. How different, she thought, and how wonderful!

The largest building in Rich Bar was the two-story Empire Hotel. It was built of rough planks. Its roof was covered with canvas. The Empire was where Dame Shirley and Fayette decided to spend their first days in Rich Bar.

Shirley stepped through the open doorway of the hotel. As her eyes adjusted to the darkness inside, she saw that the hotel was also a store. Lying about in great confusion were piles of clothing and bolts of red calico. Nearby were hams, dried meats, canned oysters, and other groceries.

A woman, wiping her hands as she came from behind the counter, rushed to greet Dame Shirley. She introduced herself as Louise Bancroft. Mrs. Bancroft and her husband Curtis were the owners of the Empire.

Louise Bancroft was a tiny, sturdy woman. She had come to California two years earlier, crossing the Great Plains and Rocky Mountains to strike it rich in the gold fields.

The overland route was shorter but more

dangerous than the one Dame Shirley had taken with her husband. It meant months of travel in open country. The wind and hard weather on the way took its toll. Although she was only 25, Mrs. Bancroft looked much older. Her face was yellowed by wind and sunburn. Worry lines creased her face. But the trip had also burned character and strength into her features. Dame Shirley took an instant liking to her.

For her part, Mrs. Bancroft was delighted to see Dame Shirley. She said that it was marvelous to have another woman in camp. She said this over the loud cries of her two-week-old son.

The baby had been born in the hotel. One of the other two women in Rich Bar had helped Mrs. Bancroft with her son's birth. Curtis was too sick to help, and when the woman who was helping also became sick, Mrs. Bancroft was on her own.

Within a few days, Louise Bancroft had gone back to work. Dame Shirley called her a woman of the West. That meant Mrs. Bancroft was tough and independent with a spirit of adventure. She and Shirley became friends.

Dame Shirley and Fayette spent the next few days looking for a permanent place to live. Nothing they could find in Rich Bar was much to their liking. Instead, Fayette decided to build a log cabin in the neighboring mining camp of Indian Bar.

In early October 1851, Dame Shirley and Fayette moved into their one-room log cabin. The ceiling of the cabin was lined with white cotton cloth. The walls were covered with calico printed with bright flowers of purple, green, and blue. Over the door hung a canvas flap. The only window had no glass. The fireplace was built of mud, stones, and sticks.

For furniture, Dame Shirley had a rough collection of odds and ends. A little pine table, covered with oilcloth, stood in one corner. The floor was so uneven that the table usually wobbled on three legs, reminding Dame Shirley constantly of a dog with a sore foot.

The cabin was altogether unlike any home either of them had ever lived in before. But this was California, and a log cabin was the next best thing to a palace in a mining camp.

About a month after moving in, Dame Shirley decided to try her hand at panning for gold. She knew the miners often played tricks on newcomers. They would "salt" an area with gold dust, then laugh when the newcomer made an instant "strike." Having no intention of being played for such a greenhorn, Dame Shirley kept her plans a secret.

On a cool November morning, Dame Shirley left her cabin looking very much like a proper New England lady out for a Sunday stroll. Her hands were snug inside a new pair of white kid gloves. A pretty parasol rested on her shoulder. She didn't look the least bit like someone about to go panning for gold.

Dame Shirley strolled casually toward the river. She could hear the sounds of the miners working their claims. They shouted to one another over the roar of the rushing stream and over the noise of their digging.

Dame Shirley was amazed at the many different languages she heard on her way through camp—English, French, Chinese, Italian, Russian, Spanish. The whole world seemed to have rushed to California!

Dame Shirley had heard the other miners call all the Spanish-speaking miners "Spaniards." But she knew better. Few, if any, were from Spain. Most were either from Mexico or were native *Californios*. Others were from Chile, Peru, and other Latin American countries.

Many of the Hispanic miners had mined elsewhere before coming to California. They brought with them excellent mining skills and superior equipment. This made many white miners jealous. Few of them had ever mined anywhere before rushing to California with gold fever. They had been shopkeepers, farmers, teachers, sailors, factory workers—nearly everything *but* miners.

All of the miners, no matter where they were from, had the same dream. They wanted to find as much gold as possible and then return home with their newly found riches. They'd all heard tales of men who had come to California and become wealthy overnight. In pursuit of instant wealth, the miners worked from dawn to dusk. They stood in icy-cold streams, washing out pan after pan of sand and gravel, hoping to find gold.

Dame Shirley watched these men pursue their dream as she walked. Soon she came upon a deep hole with a group of sweating miners in it. The miners were dressed in shirts of bright red or blue flannel. They wore their black trousers tucked into the tops of tall leather boots. On their heads were black felt hats with broad brims.

They also wore a good deal of the riverbank. Dirt flew with each stroke, landing in a light shower on them as they worked. Sunlight flashed from the picks and shovels as they tore into the river bank. Dame Shirley watched with great interest as the miners washed their "pay dirt" in shallow pans.

As she watched, she stepped slowly toward the edge of the hole. She looked at them from beneath her parasol. Begging their pardon for interrupting, she asked if they might allow her to try her hand at panning.

At first the dark-bearded men just looked up at Dame Shirley. Then one of the miners

shrugged his shoulders and bent to fill a pan with dirt, which he passed up to Dame Shirley.

She carried it to the river's edge and knelt down. Dipping the pan in the icy water, she gently swirled it about in a circular motion. She repeated the actions of the miners just as she'd seen them doing. The dirt and sand washed over the side of the pan. Soon, nothing was left in the pan but several tiny, gleaming particles of gold.

Several times she returned for more pans to try. In the process, she spoiled her new gloves, froze her fingers, soaked her feet, tore her dress, and lost some jewelry to the river's swift current. For her trouble, Shirley obtained gold worth a total of three dollars and twenty-five cents! This was certainly not any way to get rich, she thought. Why, in San Francisco you couldn't even get handkerchiefs laundered for that!

Dame Shirley's "success" was actually typical of most miners. To be sure, now and then someone would make a "lucky strike." One miner took out gold worth two hundred and fifty-six dollars from a single pan. But such luck was rare. Most miners averaged no more than six to eight dollars a day—about what they would have earned in two or three days had they stayed at their jobs back home.

Because gold mining was such a risky business, the miners tended to move frequently. When rumors of a rich strike would sweep through a mining camp, the miners would pull up stakes and rush off in a dozen different directions. Boom towns quickly turned into ghost towns.

Many mining camps also were abandoned temporarily during the winter months. Heavy rains made it too difficult to mine. The rivers became swollen and angry. The miners drifted into San Francisco or Sacramento to wait for spring.

Dame Shirley wrote about all of this to her sister. Most other accounts of the Gold Rush that found their way back East were filled with Gold Fever myths. Dame Shirley's letters were the first true account of the Gold Rush, even if they only had a readership of one.

During the winter of 1851–1852, the rains

came early and hard along the Feather River. Travel over the steep mountain roads was soon impossible. Few miners were able to leave. Most were forced to spend the winter in the mining camps.

Dame Shirley observed some unpleasant changes in the miners as the gloomy winter months dragged by. They became bored and edgy. Dame Shirley thought this was only natural. The miners, after all, had no work to do. Nor did they have any newspapers, churches, or theaters. They didn't even have any female companionship!

The one thing the miners did have, Dame Shirley noticed, was plenty of whiskey. She was disturbed that so many of the miners—who otherwise were fine young men—became not just foolish but mean when they were drunk.

The worst bout of drinking began on Christmas Eve. For three days and nights the miners drank. Dame Shirley and Fayette stayed in their cabin, afraid to go outside. They could hear the drunken miners dancing and howling. Some barked like dogs. Others roared like bulls. Still others hissed like snakes and geese. The two New Englanders had never heard such strange noises coming from people before. They also heard gunshots and fights.

Dame Shirley looked forward to the coming of spring. She hoped that things would settle down once the men began mining again.

Unfortunately, spring brought with it new problems. Dame Shirley was distressed by the growing bad feelings between the white miners and the "Spaniards."

As mining resumed in the spring, the whites became increasingly jealous of the Hispanic miners. The white miners resented the fine equipment and better skills of the Hispanics. The white miners passed a rule that no "foreigners" could mine in Rich Bar. This rule angered the Hispanic miners, but other than move to nearby Indian Bar there wasn't much they could do about it. One evening in late April, an Hispanic miner and a white miner got into an argument. The white miner owed money to the Hispanic miner. Unwilling to pay up, he ended the argument by stabbing the Spaniard in the chest. The Spaniard survived, but nothing was done to punish the man who attacked him. Dame Shirley thought the whole affair was atrocious. She wrote her sister and told her about how little law there was in the camps. This was part of the horrible truth about life in the diggings. It was a truth that didn't often find its way East.

Dame Shirley blamed her fellow countrymen for the growing problems in the mining camps. Yet she also believed that most of the miners were kind and sensible men. They had come to California with high hopes. They worked hard, day after day, in a desperate search for gold. But they had little to show for their labors.

Never before had Dame Shirley seen men under such circumstances. Her life in New England had not prepared her for what she witnessed in California. She tried her best to be understanding. And, indeed, she understood very well the deep frustration of the miners. She also understood—but could not accept—their jealousy and violence.

4

Celebration and Farewell

Dame Shirley rose early on the morning of July 4, 1852. She wanted to put the finishing touches on the flag she had made for the day's celebration of American independence. She checked the seams along the red calico stripes. She added a few more stitches to the large star sewn onto the blue field.

By six o'clock, she was on her way to Rich Bar where the day's festivities were to be held.

After breakfast at the Empire Hotel, Dame Shirley helped with the decorations. She watched proudly as her home-made American flag was raised to the top of a tall pine tree in front of the hotel. Inside, she helped decorate the dining room with grapevines and bunches of flowers.

By ten o'clock, the preparations were complete. Dame Shirley and Mrs. Bancroft took their places of honor on the porch of the hotel. The miners gathered in the dusty street to cheer the patriotic speeches of the day. Then everyone retired to the hotel dining room for a hearty meal, songs, and more celebrating.

The miners raised their glasses in toasts to American independence. Dame Shirley found many of the toasts amusing. But she also recalled how the Christmas celebration had gotten out of hand when the drinking began.

In the early evening, Shirley and Fayette returned to their cabin in Indian Bar. Just as they reached their doorway, they heard shouts back in Rich Bar. "Down with the Spaniards!" someone yelled.

"The great American people forever!" cried another.

The Hispanic and white miners were engaged in a fierce battle. Two or three Hispanic miners were seriously injured.

The sounds of the battle soon passed. Dame Shirley and Fayette sat at the wobbly table in their cabin. Some of the injured would surely be brought to Fayette to have their wounds tended to. While they waited for the wounded, Dame Shirley helped Fayette get ready. Then they poured themselves some tea and stared glumly out their window.

The fighting between the Hispanic miners and the white miners surprised no one. Bad feelings between the two groups had continued to grow throughout the spring and summer. Writing to her sister, Shirley noted that the violence had erupted because seven or eight white Rich Bar miners were "drunk with whisky and patriotism."

Drinking and violence remained a problem all through the summer. Dame Shirley told her sister that this was because gamblers ruled the mines. These were "reckless, bad men" who encouraged drinking because it made it easier for them to take advantage of the miners. They also encouraged the white miners to blame their troubles on the Hispanic miners.

As a result, hardly a week passed when there wasn't some kind of drunken fight among the miners. Dame Shirley, who often witnessed the bloody results of these combats, sadly concluded that the rest of the people were afraid of the gamblers. At any rate, even the most glaring injustices against the Hispanic miners passed "unnoticed."

In the week that followed Independence Day, Dame Shirley tried to put these troubling thoughts out of her mind. She turned her attention to the beauties of the countryside.

On Sunday afternoon, July 11, she visited one of her favorite spots along the river. It was a little meadow covered with wild flowers. On this warm summer's day, she found it filled with magnificent butterflies. Some were shiny and black, splashed with orange. Others were purple and fringed with gold. Still others were yellow and blue, pink, white, and even green.

Dame Shirley walked back to her cabin, refreshed by the beauties she had seen. In her arms, she carried great bundles of wild flowers. When she reached her cabin, she began arranging the flowers in jars, bottles, and pails. She sang softly to herself as she worked.

Suddenly, the air was filled with shouts from Rich Bar. Cries of "Down with the Spaniards!" once again echoed off the forested hills.

A second or two later, Dame Shirley heard a deep groan from just outside her cabin. Then someone said, "Why Tom, poor fellow, are you really wounded?"

Dame Shirley rushed to the door but before she reached it, someone kicked it open. A miner burst in asking to see Dr. Clappe. Dame Shirley could see her husband approaching. She directed the miner to lay the wounded man down. The miner explained hurriedly that his young friend Tom Somers had just been stabbed. Assisted by Dame Shirley, Fayette did what he could for the injured man. But within fifteen minutes, Somers was dead.

Dame Shirley and Fayette learned that earlier that day, Somers had attacked an Hispanic miner named Domingo. Domingo had stabbed Somers in self-defense. But the trouble wasn't over. More shouts and yells reached the cabin.

"Drive every foreigner off the river!" someone shouted. "Don't let one of the murderous devils remain!"

Shirley heard a loud splash from the river. Then gunshots rang out. Having been discovered, Domingo had dived into the river to escape. A mob of white miners were in hot pursuit.

The whites fired eight or ten shots at Domingo as he swam furiously across the water. When he reached the other side, he ran like an antelope up the bank. Several men continued the chase, but they could not overtake him.

The white miners placed the blame for the whole affair on the Hispanic miners. They formed a Committee of Vigilance and arrested five or six Hispanic miners. The Committee sentenced two of them to be whipped and ordered the others to leave the area that evening.

Dame Shirley was sickened by these events. The two Hispanic miners were tied to posts. They were lashed with leather whips. Dame Shirley refused to watch.

When the first blow fell, Dame Shirley tried

to block out the fearful sounds of the snapping whip and the tortured screams of the men. She knew that she would never be able to erase from her memory the horror of this moment. She had heard of such things, but not until this instant had she believed that men could actually beat other human beings like this. She turned away in disgust.

By the fall of 1852, the search for gold in Rich Bar and Indian Bar was almost over. The miners were leaving for places where they hoped they would have better luck. They certainly didn't want to spend another winter on the Feather River. By early November, only about twenty miners remained in Indian Bar.

Fayette and Dame Shirley were also thinking about leaving. There wasn't much need for a doctor anymore in these deserted mining camps. She wrote Mary Jane that "the whole world (*our* world) was, to use a phrase much in vogue here, 'dead broke.'"

As the days grew cooler, Dame Shirley sat

for hours at a time on a box in the chimney corner of her cabin. She held her chin in her hand, rocking backwards and forwards. Fayette had gone off to tend to a sick friend on the American River.

In the meantime, the express man with whom they had arranged to move from Indian Bar came and went. Snow and freezing rain fell from the cloud-covered sky. The mountain passes might close at any time. It was getting dangerous, and the express man had refused to wait.

To make matters worse, their cabin was falling apart. Rain poured through leaks in the roof. Mud covered everything. The overhead lining was stained. The cloth on the walls was faded and torn.

By the time Fayette returned, a snow storm had indeed closed the passes. No mule trains or wagons could get through. The snow was five feet deep in places. The man who brought this news offered Dame Shirley his horse. Fayette and the miners who wanted to leave would have to walk.

It was late November. There would be no fresh supplies until spring. To stay longer would be to risk starvation. Dame Shirley and Fayette decided that it was time for them to go.

On the night before their departure, the skies over Indian Bar cleared. Dame Shirley walked at midnight through the nearly empty mining camp. In the moonlight, she gazed one last time at the snow-covered hills and the icy river. She once had called herself a "thistle-seed," ready to blow wherever the wind might take her. That restlessness was now stilled.

Dame Shirley felt both joy and sadness as she stood in the cold mountain air. Here she had faced many hardships and dangers. She had seen life at its most brutal. She didn't yet understand all that had happened to her during the fourteen months she had lived among these rough men in this narrow mountain canyon. All she knew for certain was that she had discovered a strength within herself that she had never known before.

Epilogue

The Gold Rush was a turning point in California history. It brought hundreds of thousands of people to the state. Small towns became great cities. Businesses of all sorts boomed. New forms of transportation developed. Farming and ranching greatly expanded to feed the newcomers. It seemed as though everything in California was changed by the Gold Rush.

It was also a major event in the life of Dame Shirley. She, too, was changed.

After leaving Feather River, Dame Shirley became something of a local celebrity when her letters to her sister were published in San Francisco. People admired the letters for their true-to-life details and colorful incidents.

Hers was undoubtedly the best account of life in the mines. Other writers used her letters as the basis for their own stories. Bret Harte borrowed freely from them in his writings about the Gold Rush. And so, some say, did Mark Twain.

Dame Shirley's marriage to Fayette broke up when they returned to San Francisco. He moved on to Hawaii; Dame Shirley stayed in California.

In 1854, Dame Shirley became a teacher in the San Francisco public schools. She taught for the next twenty-four years. Following her retirement in 1878, she returned to the East. She died there at the age of 85.

Long after her death, Dame Shirley's fame has been kept alive by her letters and through the memories of her students. She had been a very popular teacher in San Francisco. On Saturdays, she often took her students on outings. Sometimes she would take them to the ocean along the city's western border. There they would wade in the surf and take hikes along the beach. In the evening they would roast potatoes in campfires on the sand. They would sing and play games.

The best part of these outings was usually saved for last. Dame Shirley would gather her students around her. "I've got a few stories for you," she would begin. They could see the sparkle in her eyes, even in the fading glow of twilight. They knew that the stories she was about to tell were true. They listened quietly as Dame Shirley told them about her adventures long ago in the mining camps of the California Gold Rush.

Afterword

The Shirley Letters provided the research for much of the story we have told here. All conversations shown in quotation marks were the actual words and thoughts recorded by Dame Shirley in her letters about the Gold Rush days.

Notes

Page 3 On January 24, 1848, James Wilson Marshall discovered gold in the south fork of the American River at Sutter's Mill near Coloma, California. By May, the news had swept through San Francisco, and the Gold Rush was underway! Caught up in the spell of gold fever, thousands of men abandoned the cities and towns up and down the coast of California.

Then news reached places beyond California. By 1849 people from all over the world had quit their jobs and left their families to seek their fortunes in the California mountains. Some of these Forty-Niners, as they were called, found gold, but most did not. Among those who did *not* get rich were James Marshall, who first discovered gold in California, and John Sutter, who owned the land on which Marshall made his discovery.

The California Gold Rush reached its peak in 1853 when more than $63 million worth of gold was produced. In 1859, with the discovery of rich silver deposits in Nevada, most of the remaining miners left California, putting an end to the Gold Rush.

Page 4 Fayette spent less time practicing medicine than he had expected. There were two reasons for this. First, he hadn't been the only doctor who thought there was a shortage of doctors in the gold country. By the time Fayette arrived quite a few rival doctors were already practicing. Second, Fayette was not immune to gold fever himself and frequently disappeared in pursuit of a claim of his own. He failed to strike it rich either as a doctor or a miner.

Page 5 Mules are the offspring of a male donkey and a female horse. They look somewhat like horses, but have a donkey's long ears, short mane, small feet, short tail, and braying voice. Mules are hardy and strong animals. They are able to work hard over long periods of time. Mules are also very sure-footed. They need less water than horses and travel nearly as fast.

Page 10 The names of many of the mining camps in California ended in *Bar*. The California bars were ridges of sand or gravel that looked like river islands. Many contained gold. In the words of Dame Shirley, "these bars are formed by deposits of earth, rolling down from the mountains, crowding the river aside and occupying a portion of its deserted bed."

Page 23 Thousands of people made the dangerous overland journey across the Great Plains and the Rocky Mountains to California. Groups of travelers banded together to form wagon trains. In the spring of 1849, hundreds of wagon trains headed west from such towns as St. Joseph or Independence, Missouri; Council Bluffs, Iowa; and Fort Smith, Arkansas. Some followed trails that had already been established—the old Oregon, Mormon, Santa Fe, and Los Angeles trails. Others blazed new paths westward. The journey to California sometimes took as long as eight months. The wagon trains had to cross mountains and deserts. Many people lost their lives on the way. But the pull of gold fever was strong. By July of 1849, more than five thousand wagons had already passed through Fort Laramie, Wyoming on the way to California. Thousands more were on other trails.

Pages 26–30 Gases and liquids from beneath the earth's crust carried gold to the surface and deposited it in veins of rock. Over many millions of years, rain, wind, and snow eroded the rock. It was worn down into gravel and sand. Then gold-bearing gravel and sand were washed into rivers. Gold is very heavy, so gold carried by rivers tended to fall wherever the river currents slowed—behind large boulders and into holes and cracks in the riverbed. Gold of this sort is called "placer gold." It takes the form of dust, flakes, and nuggets.

Most of the gold mined in California from 1848 to 1850 was placer gold. Dame Shirley saw miners "panning" for placer gold. The miners used a pan they called a "washbowl." The washbowl looked like a large pie pan, but with deeper sides.

The miners scooped up sand, gravel, and water into the washbowl. Then they swirled the water to make a little whirlpool, carefully spilling water, sand, and gravel over the rim of the pan. Any gold mixed in with the sand and gravel would sink to the bottom of the pan. Many miners never did master the trick of swirling. Because of this, they may have lost gold over the washbowl rim or abandoned claims they thought were worthless.

Page 31 Many miners earned about the same or only a little more than they would have at home.

They found that their money couldn't buy as much in California as it did back home. Some people made fortunes during the Gold Rush by selling overpriced goods to the miners. In 1849, two miners bought one box of sardines for $16, one pound of hard bread for $2, one pound of butter for $6, one half-pound of cheese for $3, and two bottles of ale for $16. This was their food supply for the day. Eggs often sold at $4 per dozen but could sometimes cost as much as $3 each! Potatoes sold for $3 a pound, and candles $1 each. One miner bought a needle and two spools of thread for $7.50. The cost of flour could be as high as $800 per barrel, and onions could fetch a price of $2 apiece.

Pages 33–34 There was almost no law and order in the mining camps. Instead, miners enforced their own ideas of justice by driving "troublemakers" out of town, hanging or shooting some suspected criminals, and whipping others. Punishment was swift and often unfair. The people who decided that the "wrongdoers" were guilty and then punished them, were often the same people who had accused them in the first place.

Miners also passed "laws" like the one that outlawed "foreigners." It was applied to Hispanic miners even though some of them were native to California. Their families had come to California when it belonged to Mexico or even earlier when it belonged to Spain.

Prejudice in the mines was widespread, and it grew uglier as the Gold Rush played itself out. Hispanic miners, Chinese miners, and American Indian miners were often cheated, beaten, robbed, or run out of town. At times, unsuccessful white miners attacked nonwhites who had found success in the mines. Sometimes the attacks were made just so that white miners could steal already mined gold or to drive "foreigners" off land where gold had been found.

Jim Rawls lives in California and teaches at Diablo Valley College. In addition to *Dame Shirley and the Gold Rush* and *Never Turn Back,* Mr. Rawls is the author of a number of scholarly works.